WHO WOULD WIN?™

TYRANNOSAURUS REX

vs.

VELOCIRAPTOR

BY
JERRY PALLOTTA

ILLUSTRATED BY
ROB BOLSTER

Scholastic Inc.
New York   Toronto   London   Auckland
Sydney   Mexico City   New Delhi   Hong Kong

Author note:
T. rex and velociraptor lived on different continents, millions of
years apart. But what might have happened if they met?

To T. rex Nancy and T. rex Alex and their little velociraptors
Brittany, Meaghan, Nick, and Tim.
—*J.P.*

To my Tyrannaboyus rex—William.
—*R.B.*

Text copyright © 2010 by Jerry Pallotta
Illustrations copyright © 2010 by Rob Bolster

ISBN 978-0-545-17573-9

60 59   22

Printed in the U.S.A. 40
This edition first printing, January 2016

Book design by Rob Bolster

Let's go back millions of years.

What would happen if a Tyrannosaurus rex and a velociraptor met each other? What if both of these dinosaurs were hungry? What if they had a fight? Who do you think would win?

PTEROSAURS

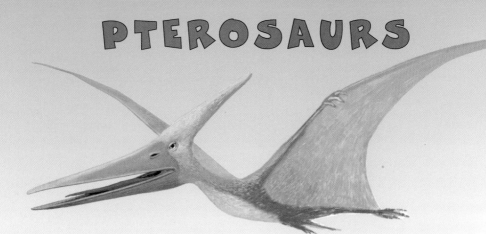

Millions of years ago, three types of huge creatures lived on earth. Pterosaurs flew in the sky.

PLESIOSAURS

Plesiosaurs swam in the ocean.

DINOSAURS

Dinosaurs walked on land.

> **DEFINITION**
> *Dinosaur means "terrifying lizard."*

Some dinosaurs walked on two legs, while others walked on four.

Today, pterosaurs, plesiosaurs, and dinosaurs are extinct, which means they died out.

SCIENTIFIC NAME:
**Tyrannosaurus rex means "tyrant lizard king."
For short, let's call him T. rex.**

Meet Tyrannosaurus rex. It had a huge head, sharp teeth, big back legs, and teeny front arms. Just looking at one is scary! No one really knows what color it was. What do you think?

FUN FACT
*Lizards today come in many colors—
some even can change color!
Tyrannosaurus rex could have been
almost any color.*

QUESTION
*Were they hot pink?
Probably not!*

WHAT IF?
*Maybe they were green, like an
iguana of today.*

SCIENTIFIC NAME:
**Velociraptor means "speedy thief."
Let's call him raptor.**

Meet velociraptor. Paleontologists think it looked like this. Velociraptor seems to be built for speed and quick attack.

FUN FACT
A paleontologist studies prehistoric life.

INTERESTING FACT
Prehistoric means "before recorded history."

T. rex was discovered in modern times by people who found its fossils. Here is a photograph of the excavation site where this T. rex was found.

DEFINITION
A fossil is the preserved remains of a dead plant or animal.

FUN FACT
The largest and most complete T. rex skeleton discovered is named Sue. It was found by and named after Sue Hendrickson, a paleontologist.

Raptors were discovered the same way. Geologists and paleontologists found their fossilized bones.

DID YOU KNOW?
A geologist studies the history of earth in its rocks.

BONUS FACT
A new generation of dinosaur hunters has been looking for dinosaur DNA.

This raptor fossil was found next to a protoceratops that it was fighting. Both dinosaurs died in this real-life "Who Would Win?"

Here is a full T. rex skeleton. When scientists assembled its fossilized bones, they learned that T. rex walked on two legs.

INTERESTING FACT

A newborn T. rex skeleton has never been discovered. Maybe you will be the person who unearths it.

DID YOU KNOW?

Fossilized T. rex footprints have never showed tail marks. This indicates that T. rex did not drag its tail while walking or running.

Here is a full raptor skeleton. Its fossilized bones look skinnier and more mobile than the T. rex skeleton.

T. rex had a huge jaw with more than fifty teeth. Its teeth were not designed for eating vegetables. It had carnivore teeth, as sharp as knives.

DINO TRIVIA
When dinosaur fossils were first found in China, people thought they were ancient dragon bones.

T. rex had a small brain. What did it think about?

The raptor also had a mouthful of sharp teeth. That means it was a meat eater, too.

QUESTION

Would you want to be this dinosaur's dentist?

REMEMBER

Proportionally, a raptor has a larger brain than a T. rex.

A raptor's teeth point inward to trap its prey.

Some scientists think that T. rex was a brutal hunter. It had the size, teeth, and design to be an apex predator. It is hard to believe that any animal would want to challenge a T. rex.

DEFINITION
An apex predator is an animal that has no natural enemies.

GROSS FACT
Carrion is the rotting body of a dead animal.

Other scientists think that T. rex was not aggressive, but was a carrion eater. Instead of hunting, it roamed for animals that were already dead.

The raptor was a predator that most likely hunted and ate smaller animals. It probably hunted in packs. Scientists think it hunted by ambushing its prey.

> **DEFINITION**
> *An ambush is an*
> *attack by surprise.*

WHAT DO YOU THINK?

A group of raptors: Should we call them a bunch, a gang, a pack, a flock, a clique, a crash, a rumble, a storm, a herd, or something else?

T. REX FOOT

Boom! Boom! Boom! That is what a walking T. rex sounded like. The ground would shake, alerting nearby animals. *Boom! Boom! Boom!*

One toe
(horse)

Two toes
(sloth)

Three toes
(rhinoceros)

QUESTION:
How is a T. rex like a chicken?

ANSWER:
They both have four toes on each foot.

Four toes
(chicken)

Five toes
(human)

RAPTOR FOOT

Paleontologists think the raptor was sneaky and quiet as it walked. A raptor probably tiptoed before attacking. It differs from other dinosaurs because it had a sickle on each foot.

SICKLE THEORY #1

Did the raptor use its sickles to slash and cut its prey?

SICKLE THEORY #2

Or were sickles used as grips to climb trees? Was the raptor a tree climber? What do you think?

T. REX ARMS

The small arms of a T. rex seem almost useless. What could it do with them? A T. rex had only two fingers on each hand. In a football game, the T. rex would fumble the ball.

RAPTOR ARMS

HANDY FACT

People have nails on their fingers and toes. Dinosaurs had claws. The hands of a raptor have huge claws.

GROSS FACT

A raptor's arms and hands seem perfect for a dinosaur that is an aggressive hunter—quick, long, and strong. A raptor could easily rip apart its prey.

Raptors had three fingers on each hand. The middle finger was the longest, and the first finger was the shortest.

TYRANNOSAURUS REX TAIL

INTERESTING FACT

T. rex walked on two legs, its tail balancing its body and huge head.

The T. rex used its tail for balancing, but it may have also used it as a weapon. Getting whacked by its whip-tail could not have been fun.

VELOCIRAPTOR TAIL

DINO TRIVIA
The largest raptor ever discovered is the Utahraptor. It is twenty feet long.

DINOSAUR TAILS

ANKYLOSAURUS
CLUBBED

POLACANTHUS
JAGGED

STEGOSAURUS
SPIKED

Some dinosaur experts now think the raptor's tail may have been straight and stiff.

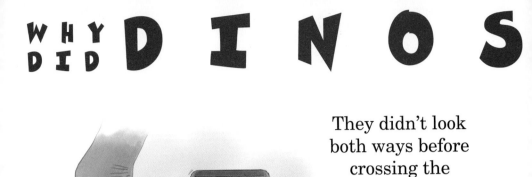

They didn't look both ways before crossing the street.

They texted while driving.

One skateboard stunt too many.

Too many video
games turned their
brains to mush.

They liked to climb up
trees, but didn't know
how to climb down.

Aliens from other
galaxies went hunting
on earth and wiped out
all of the dinosaurs.

SCIENTIFIC THEORIES OF DINOSAUR EXTINCTION

Asteroid Collision

A giant meteor hit earth and changed its climate.

Rise of Small Animals

Small sneaky animals started eating dinosaur eggs faster than new eggs could be hatched.

Food Chain Imbalance

The larger dinosaurs had trouble finding enough food and started eating each other.

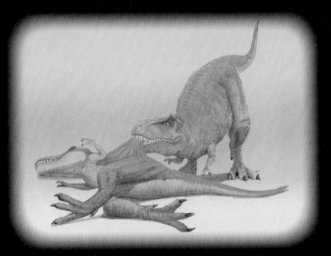

Heavy Volcanic Activity

So much soot and dust erupted into the air that sunshine was blocked and plants died. The plant eaters didn't have enough to eat. Eventually the meat eaters had no plant eaters to eat.

Ice Age

The earth became too cold.

Disease

New infections, colds, and viruses attacked the dinosaurs.

What if a T. rex had a fight with a raptor? Who do you think would win?

Here comes a T. rex to face off with the raptor. It's not a fair fight. The T. rex is much bigger. But the raptor doesn't seem to be afraid. It does not run away. The raptor must have a secret.

Just as the T. rex is about to fight, the quick raptor leaps onto its back. The raptor slices the T. rex with its sickles. The angry T. rex bucks, and the raptor gets flung into the air.

INTERESTING FACT

A raptor was only about 3 to 4 feet high—not much taller than a third grader!

The raptor gets right back up and jumps on the T. rex's tail. It slashes the T. rex but gets knocked to the ground again.

The raptor starts making a squeaking sound. The T. rex charges the little dinosaur. This time the T. rex is fed up. "Squeak! Squeak!" cries the raptor.

The raptor gets out its message.
A pack of raptors comes to the
rescue. The T. rex steps on
one, then rips it with its
teeth. But now the
T. rex is in trouble.

What seemed like an easy fight has turned into a battle
for survival. One, two, or even three raptors are no
problem. But more than ten?

The raptor pack slashes and cuts the T. rex. It's over! The T. rex crashes to the ground. It makes no sense to fight a pack animal.

If it was a one-on-one fight, the huge T. rex would easily beat a raptor. But nature doesn't always present a fair fight.

WHO HAS THE ADVANTAGE?
CHECKLIST

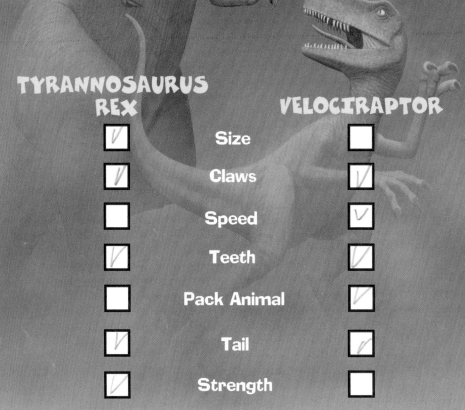

TYRANNOSAURUS REX		VELOCIRAPTOR
☑	Size	☐
☑	Claws	☑
☐	Speed	☑
☑	Teeth	☑
☐	Pack Animal	☑
☑	Tail	☑
☑	Strength	☐

Author note: This is one way the fight might have ended.
How would you write the ending?